C000002145

English Heritage welcomes you to Framlingham Castle

Framlingham castle lies to the north of the town, beyond the parish church. The castle has thirteen towers linked together with high curtain walls – you can walk safely all the way round the battlements. Within the walls are an attractive group of brick and flint buildings, built as a school and poorhouse, but now housing displays of local history and a shop.

There is a small car park just in front of the castle, but coaches should park further away in the town. Toilet facilities are available within the castle as well as in the town. There are good places for picnicking around the castle walls, particularly in the Lower Court to the left of the entrance gateway.

ABOVE *The Poorhouse of three dates – the brick workhouse on the left (1664), the central range of 1729, and the north wing on the right.*

Contents

For Orford Castle, please turn to page 22

LOWER CO

Prison Tower

Castle Ditch

N

Principal Dates in Framlingham's History

1101 Roger Bigod given the manor	1547 Castle seized by Henry VIII
1140 Hugh Bigod probably builds first castle	1553 Queen Mary's headquarters before her accession
1157 Castle surrendered to Henry II	1635 Sold to Sir Robert Hitcham
1173 First castle demolished	1664 Brick Workhouse
1189 Roger Bigod II probably rebuilds castle	1729 Poorhouse rebuilt
1216 Captured by king John after short siege	1913 Becomes an Ancient Monument in State guardianship
1309 Death of last Bigod	
Thereafter occupied by Mowbray and Howard dukes of Norfolk until	

Tour of Framlingham Castle

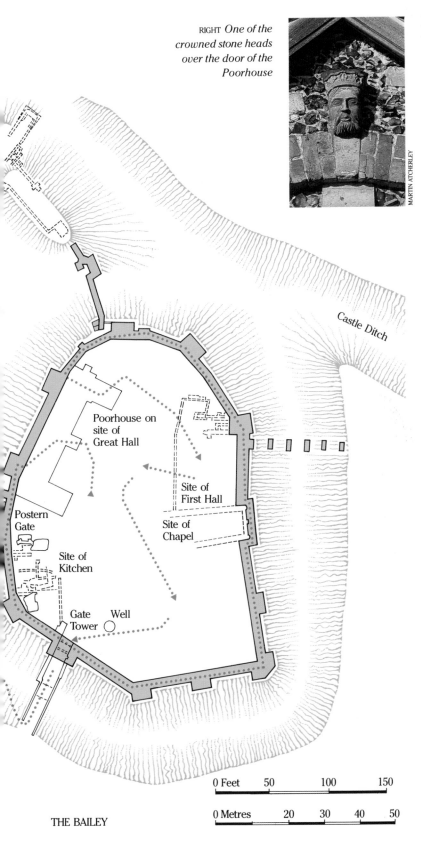

MARTIN ATCHERLEY

Poorhouse

The tour starts at the shop where you probably bought this guide. Built long after the castle had fallen into ruin, the Poorhouse was for children only at first. It was rebuilt in 1729 for up to a hundred adult paupers – notice the two large fireplaces at the other end of the room, one above another, showing that there were two floors as well as attics above the present ceiling. Here is kept the parish fire engine, bought in 1844; it was hand-propelled and hand-pumped.

The three lower small windows belong to the Norman hall which stood here before the poorhouse was built. These openings could be wide because this side of the castle was protected from attack by the outer defences. You can see these through the windows, but there is a much finer view from the wall walk.

If you have a few minutes to wait here, notice the way that the entrance doors are closed by falling weights, and the carved stone head over the outside of the door, wearing a coronet. There are other heads over the windows, and they come from some late medieval building in the castle now destroyed.

Wall Walk

The Wall Walk is reached by climbing the spiral staircase next to the shop. Look up at the late medieval doorframes and the vaulting above you. The spiral stair itself is unusual in that it rises anti-clockwise. Most castle stairs corkscrew up the other way so that an attacker climbing the stairs could not wield his sword properly in his right hand. Consequently a defender standing above would be at an advantage. But here at Framlingham this staircase was the only permanent access to the wall walk, and it would be more likely to be defenders, rushing to man the wall walk and towers, who would be climbing the stairs rather than attackers. Any attackers who got inside the castle would be assaulting the other buildings rather than trying to regain the wall walk.

As you reach the top of the stairs, notice the light timberframed back wall of the **tower** (11). All thirteen towers are very similar, usually with open backs and wooden gangways across the gaps they made in the wall walk. These gangways could be removed by the defenders when any attackers had succeeded in getting on to the battlements. Then the attackers could neither fight their way right round the wall walk (as we are doing), nor dominate the interior of the castle.

Castle Ditch

Poorhouse on site of Great Hall

Site of First Hall

Postern Gate

Site of Chapel

Site of Kitchen

Gate Tower   Well

0 Feet   50   100   150

0 Metres   20   30   40   50

THE BAILEY

ENGLISH HERITAGE

Each of these Norman towers had a **fighting-gallery** at its very top, reached by a ladder from the level of the wall walk. The drawing opposite shows one of the towers being defended against an attack. Most of the towers are fitted up with ornamental **Tudor chimneys**, elaborately made of specially-moulded bricks in various patterns, some of which are shown in the photographs. Only one or two of the chimneys have proper fireplaces underneath. Most of them are dummies, put up to give passers-by the impression that this was a great Tudor mansion, not a modest conversion of an old castle into sets of lodgings. The small ferns are deliberately encouraged to grow, since they need sheltered stone as a habitat – and there isn't much natural stone in Suffolk.

Nowadays there is one-way traffic round the wall walk. To avoid congestion the section immediately above the poorhouse is closed to the public, but you can see what it is like through the doorway to the right at the top of the stairs. Of course in the Middle Ages men could move in either direction to defend any threatened section of wall. The roof above you is modern, but the tiles are hung from the rafters by wooden pegs in the medieval fashion. Talking of tiles, look at the roofs of the poorhouse to the left, and the complicated interlacing of the rows of tiles at the roof junctions.

Part of the view to the right is shown here. The flat area is the **Lower Court**, an outer area of the castle which provided extra space for men and horses inside a ditch and bank topped by a wooden palisade or fence. It was probably the bailey or enclosure of the first castle here, the rest being destroyed when the castle was remodelled with stone walls and towers. The square stone **Prison Tower** (to the left of the Lower Court) protected a staircase which rose between the parallel walls to a postern or small doorway immediately below where you are standing now. A postern was used instead of opening the main entrance so that a few people could enter or leave one at a time. Entrances were always the most vulnerable parts of castles and, the smaller the opening, the fewer the number who could get in at once.

Beyond the Lower Court is the **Mere**, a lake formed fairly recently by damming up the river Ore and flooding the meadows. Probably the area was marshy and wet in the Middle Ages before modern drainage and farming schemes changed things. On the hill beyond the Mere is **Framlingham College**, an independent school.

OPPOSITE PAGE *An artist's impression of a tower being defended at Framlingham. Note the plank bridge inside the tower*

RIGHT *Three of the Tudor chimneys added to the Norman towers. Only one has a fireplace under-neath. The others are dummies*

BELOW *The Prison Tower, seen from above*

TOP LEFT *Looking out through a crenel over the mere. Notice the curved slot in the stone to hold the iron peg of a movable shutter*

LOWER LEFT *Modern bridge over the gap where Tower 3 was*

ABOVE *The two Tudor brick chimneys on the left of the picture were built on top of Norman stone ones, visible at lower left*

Framlingham College was founded by public subscription as a memorial to Prince Albert, Queen Victoria's consort, in 1865. The modern building on the right is used for public concerts. After the next tower of the circuit **(Tower 12)** the Norman parapet wall of the battlements survives, patched in Tudor bricks. Several of the gaps in the parapet wall (known as crenels) have holes in their sides near the top and the outside of the walls. These holes took the ends of iron pegs which supported wooden shutters which hung in the crenel to protect men standing on the wall walk. When a defender wanted to see – or shoot – out, he pushed the lower edge of the shutter outward and upward, letting it fall back into place when he had finished. The hole at one side of the crenel has a curved slot leading into it, so that the shutter could be taken out of its sockets for repair or storage. Such a hole can be seen in the top left photograph on this page. Wood lasts longer if it is kept dry, so the shutters may have been dismantled in peacetime.

The next two towers **(Towers 13 and 1)** have shafts for latrines in one corner, with slits for ventilation in the wall above. Tower 1 is above the entrance gateway, and below you are the slots to each side down which the

portcullis would be lowered. A portcullis was an iron-shod grating which blocked the entrance passage, often behind the ordinary doors, which was hauled up above the passage when not in use. It was more difficult to force open a portcullis than doors, because it had to be lifted bodily. A wedge put into the top of a portcullis slot by a defender would make the portcullis immovable, however big a lever or manpower the attackers tried.

Inside the entrance, the low circular brick wall surrounds the castle **well**. The drawing (opposite) shows what the castle would have looked like from here at about the time of king John, with the main hall and kitchen on the left, linked by a corridor to the older hall and chapel on the right.

Beyond the entrance tower there are steeply-plunging arrowslits at the foot of the parapet wall. **Tower 3** has collapsed, its position being marked by the steps (down, then up again) in the wall walk. We do not know why this tower fell down, but old engravings show that it had a large number of arrowslits cut through its walls, and they may have weakened it. The next tower marks a right-angle turn in the wall walk. This is the only sharp corner in the circuit, and there seems to be no reason for it. But it may have been designed to protect a keep or donjon (great tower) here inside the curtain walls, like that at Orford and elsewhere, protected by the line from Tower 2 to Tower 6. But so many hundreds of cartloads of stone and earth were taken out of the castle in the early nineteenth century that we cannot tell whether any great tower was built. **Tower 5**, beyond the corner, is solid and not hollow like the rest. It has a very narrow arrowslit cut right through it. **Tower 6** has traces of arches in the wall, probably to remind men that here they were walking over the top of the chapel. The tower was converted into a Tudor lodging, with curving staircases on either side and a fine brick fireplace and chimney built into one side wall.

The photograph (above) of the two chimneys on the inner side of the wall walk shows how the Norman stone shafts from the hall below were extended upwards in Tudor bricks. The illustration also shows the flue openings level with the wall walk which were designed to help the updraught from the Norman fireplaces below.

Outside the castle here, the stone columns in the ditch supported a **bridge** by which the Mowbrays, earls of Norfolk in the late Middle Ages, could leave their feasting in the hall to take exercise by hunting in the deer park beyond.

Between Towers 7 and 8 are good views of the **earthwork defences** of Framlingham. The site plan on page 13 indicates the **castle ditch** (in the nearer belt of trees) and beyond it the next belt of trees and bushes conceals the ditch which ran at least part way round the town as well.

From **Tower 9** you can see the foundations of the other stone gateway to the Lower Court immediately below you, and at **Tower 10** you descend a modern wooden staircase back into the poorhouse. Halfway down the stair is an upper room, currently occupied by the Lanman collection of local history. As you leave the poorhouse, notice the large bread oven and Tudor fireplace on your left, and the old timber-framing above and around you.

LEFT *Traces of one of the arches in Tower 6 may have reminded people that they were walking over the site of a chapel*

MARTIN ATCHERLEY

ENGLISH HERITAGE

Life in a castle

This is a good point on the tour to think about what you have seen and to try to imagine living in a castle, without the danger and excitement of a siege. Everyday life was cold and uncomfortable. There was little or no privacy for most of the inhabitants. Furniture was rudimentary, and washing and sanitary facilities pretty basic. Food was simple: locally made bread, butter and beer, beef, mutton and pork, chicken and goose, fish (near the coast).

Vegetables mainly cabbage – no potatoes yet. Torches and candles gave some artificial light, and you slept wherever you could find room. Warmth came from open fires. It was rather like continuous camping! The illustration above gives a good idea of what Framlingham Castle must have looked like 700 years ago. Much of the interior resembled a farmyard, with the stone halls and kitchen built against the curtain walls.

ABOVE *Reconstruction illustration by Alan Sorrell of the interior of Framlingham Castle in the thirteenth century, as seen from the top of the gatehouse (Tower 1)*

Courtyard

As you walk back towards the entrance, notice on your left the Tudor brick fireplaces built into the towers high above ground level. These must have warmed the upper rooms of two-storey lodgings built mainly of wood which have now vanished. The round-topped openings beyond the next tower are cut through two thicknesses of wall.

The inner part is the wall of Bigod's early Norman **Great Hall**, with two stone chimney stacks, which we saw on the wall walk. There are some traces of the Norman fireplaces below the chimney stacks, but they take some finding.

When the curtain wall was built a generation later, it was built up against the old hall wall, and the windows of the hall were extended through the new wall as well. Later still the left-hand opening (note its fine roll-moulding) was made into a doorway leading out on to the bridge across the castle ditch into the bailey (defensible enclosure) and the deerpark outside both castle and town.

Pictured on the left are the openings in the wall and a recess with the wall overhanging above. This recess was the site of the chapel, completely gone except for the imprint or 'cast' of its east wall where the later curtain wall covered it. Above is the narrow splayed Norman window, with faint traces of arches to either side. The outline of the chapel's gabled roof can be seen above. Higher up still are the angle corbels (brackets) which were added to support a later roof.

Looking across to the other side of the courtyard, three different periods of building can be seen in the **poorhouse**. On the left is the former workhouse of 1664, now a private house, with its fine brickwork and gabled roofs. To the right, the rough stonework is the remains of the second Norman hall, with a Tudor chimney-breast above. In between is the split-flint work of the 1729 poorhouse, with five alternate male and female stone heads wearing coronets over the door and windows. These are of late medieval date, and came from some other building, perhaps a remodelling of the Norman hall.

TOP LEFT *The first Norman hall, with its stone chimneys which were extended upwards in Tudor brick. Note the doorway on the left*

LOWER LEFT *The chapel window*

8

LEFT *Four stone heads from a late medieval building now built into the 1729 Poorhouse. A fifth head is reproduced on page 3*

ABOVE *The Poorhouse with, on the extreme left, the castle entrance. The stone heads are just visible above the windows and the blue door*

9

ABOVE *In this interior view, arrowloops can be seen in the parapet and cut through the walls below. The castle entrance and well are partly hidden by the tree at the centre of the picture*

Turning again towards the castle **entrance**, you can appreciate the design of a great Norman defensive screen. The photograph above shows the double-slit arrowloops halfway up the wall. Together with the later brick fireplace (centre), this suggests either that the ground has been considerably lowered, perhaps when all that rubble was removed in the early nineteenth century, or there was a wooden gallery or floored building at this level. At the battlemented wall walk there are more (but smaller) arrowloops, and the towers usually have an arrowloop on each side as well. These arrowloops can be traced on the outside but of course they are much narrower there.

The diagrams opposite show the over-lapping fields of fire through these arrowloops. These extra defences were intended to deter approach and attack on the entrance, but they are all concentrated to one side of it. A keep or donjon sited behind the wall here as the major defensive feature – a possible explanation of the sharp turn in the wall walk – may be the reason for this parade of firepower potential. The siting of the well, not very close to either hall or kitchen, also suggests that something very important was planned here, on the sunny side of the enclosure.

To the right of the entrance are the foundations of large **kitchen fireplaces** on the ground. They have tiles set on edge, to reduce the chance of them cracking because of the intense but uneven heat. **Tower 13**, next to the entrance, has a plain but complete Norman round-topped doorway high up inside with an unusual window beyond like a ship's porthole. The latrine which it both aired and lit can be seen from the outside of the castle. The large door beyond (barred off at present) led to a gallery descending by a staircase into the Prison Tower. Another doorway higher up led on to the wall walk above the gallery.

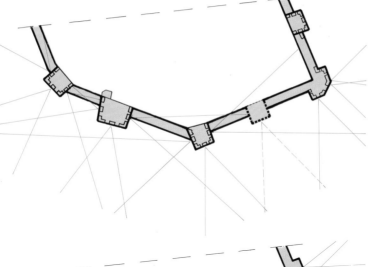

ENGLISH HERITAGE

LEFT *Fields of fire from the arrowloops at the fighting-gallery level (on tops of the towers)*

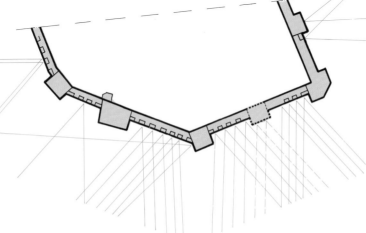

LEFT *Fields of fire from the arrowloops at the parapet level (wall walk)*

ENGLISH HERITAGE

ENGLISH HERITAGE

ABOVE *An arrowloop, seen from the outside of one of the towers*

LEFT *Fields of fire at the level of the double arrowloops (lower part of the wall)*

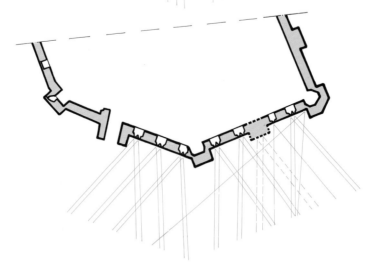

Fighting-gallery level

Wall-walk level

Lower-wall level

11

ENGLISH HERITAGE

Entrance Gateway

It may appear odd to look at this first from the inside, but this shows more clearly how it worked. The **stone pier** (or column) on the right supported a timber stair up to the room over the passage and to the wall walk, and contains a slot which guided the counterweight to the old drawbridge (see below). The **inner arch** is round-topped but the middle one, (see photograph on right), is triangular with its stones joggled together for mutual support. Such arches are unusual, but there are some others in the keep at Orford (see illustration on page 24). Just beside this arch there is a vertical groove in each side of the entrance passage down which the **portcullis** (the iron-shod grate) would be dropped to seal off the passage. The **outer arch** is Tudor, as are the wooden doors themselves. One door has a small wicket cut in it by which one man at a time could go in or out when the main doors were shut, rather like the postern door (see page 5). Note the recessed seats for porters and those awaiting admittance in the side walls. The photograph opposite shows the small oblong holes high up above the entrance, through which ran the chains or ropes which lifted the outer end of the **drawbridge** which spanned the ditch. Later the drawbridge was replaced by a permanent stone arched bridge. Over the doorway Thomas Howard, eighth duke of Norfolk (1524-47) had a carved stone panel built into the Norman masonry. This bears his **coat of arms** and, although now badly eroded by the weather, enough remains to work out the heraldry of many families associated with the castle. This is shown in the drawing on page 18.

ABOVE *The triangular arch above the Tudor doors*

ABOVE LEFT *The back of the castle gateway*

ABOVE RIGHT *The Tudor door with the Norman portcullis groove on the right*

Lower Court

If time permits, it is worth while taking the footpath walk around the outside of the castle walls. The path begins at the turning gate at the far end of the bridge (on your right as you leave the castle entrance). This path takes you down the slope of the castle ditch, past the the rough stone **Prison Tower** projecting from the main curtain walls into the **Lower Court**, which, with its high earth bank, was part of the original castle and later formed an outer defensible area. To the right you can see the three small windows of the **second castle hall** (later the poorhouse). The windows are slightly pointed at the top, the so-called 'Transitional' style between the Norman (round) and Gothic (sharply pointed) styles. The earthworks are still high and steep, and were formerly made even stronger by a wooden palisade (fence) on top of the bank.

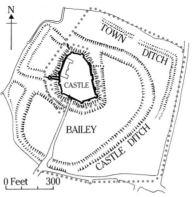

ABOVE *Two suggested walks around the outside of the castle are shown in colour on the plan and are described on this page and overleaf*

OPPOSITE PAGE *The castle gatehouse and stone bridge over the ditch*

ABOVE *The Prison Tower guarding the Lower Court*

13

ABOVE *Gateway to Lower Court, with spiral staircase*

BELOW *Columns which supported a bridge from the castle to the park*

ABOVE *The fierce face in the wall (centre of picture)*

Castle Ditches

As you pass out of the Lower Court through the stone foundation on the far side, notice the bottom of a spiral staircase, also shown in the photograph on the left. The gateway must therefore have had at least one upper floor level. If you take the footpath across the castle ditch, you will reach another outer ditch, which partly surrounded the town of Framlingham. At the corner of the field by the road is a modern fortification – a World War II pillbox or road blockhouse – on your left. Its purpose was very different and it would not have had a permanent garrison, so it is not a castle. If you turn right and follow the curving Fore Street through Framlingham, the line of the **town ditch** is on your right nearly all the way.

But if you want to stay with the castle, turn sharp right at the stone foundation and follow the footpath along the bottom of the castle ditch. This gives you an attacker's eye view of the defences. Remember that there is an outer earthwork enclosure, part of the castle, on your left as well as the stone walls on your right.

As you reach the piers (columns) which formerly supported the **bridge** leading out from the stone castle to the deerpark beyond the town, notice the elaborate Tudor brickwork of the **hall doorway** which led on to the bridge, and the window openings extended through the doubled wall thickness from the first Norman

hall. High up to the left of these openings is a fierce moustached face built into the wall (see bottom left photograph). The ditch turns sharply in front of the many-sided angle tower **(Tower 4)**. You might like to count the arrowslits between here and the gatehouse (see page 11) and enjoy the wild flowers growing on the banks here. The area is deliberately left unmown to allow the flowers and plants to thrive. Please do not pick them but leave them for others to enjoy after you. As you pass under the bridge, notice how it has been widened on either side, and then the arch itself added. Before that happened there was a gap spanned by a movable bridge, the outer end of which could be raised by ropes or chains against the outside of the entrance tower, giving it an extra protection. From this point, a short uphill climb will bring you back to the entrance, and to the car park.

Town

Framlingham is an interesting place in many ways and repays exploration. In particular the parish church of St Michael near the castle should be visited, if only to see the magnificent series of lifesize effigies, beautifully carved and painted, on the tombs of the dukes of Norfolk and others. The church has been rebuilt more than once, but the arch between the nave and the chancel remains from the late Norman period, contemporary with the castle. Framlingham's market charter goes back to 1276, and the triangular marketplace survives today surrounded by interesting buildings. A guide-book to the town is on sale in the castle shop.

ABOVE *One of the Howard tombs in St Michael's Church, Framlingham*

RIGHT *Castle hall doorway, with bridge supports*

14

RIGHT *The outside of the first castle hall, viewed from the Lower Court. The large window lights the 1729 Poorhouse. Tower 10 is on the left*

ENGLISH HERITAGE

King John hunting: a thirteenth-century miniature painting

BRITISH LIBRARY

History of Framlingham Castle

Saxons

Excavations for a drain under the path from the car park to the castle walls in 1953 uncovered 25 skeletons, some with eighth-century dress ornaments. This must be part of a Saxon cemetery.

The Bigods

The manor of Framlingham was given to Roger Bigod by king Henry I in 1101. Roger already held much land in Suffolk and when his son Hugh was created earl of Norfolk by king Stephen in 1140, it was really the old earldom of East Anglia, both Norfolk and Suffolk, which was revived. Hugh Bigod had three major castles near the east coast, at Bungay, Framlingham and Walton.

He also had a claim to the royal castle of Norwich. The only other royal castles nearer than Colchester were small ones at Eye and Haughley. Although Hugh did arrange a reconciliation between king Stephen and archbishop Theobald at Framlingham, Hugh was usually in rebellion against the Crown. When king Henry II came to the throne, Hugh Bigod's castles were surrendered to him and a royal garrison occupied Framlingham castle. King Henry II began building a new castle at Orford about 1165. Although Bungay and Framlingham castles were returned to Hugh Bigod in exchange for a heavy fine in 1165, Henry kept Walton castle until he had completed Orford castle, and then destroyed Walton.

In 1173 Henry II's eldest son rebelled against his father and was backed by a number of barons including Hugh Bigod. Haughley castle was destroyed and the city of Norwich sacked, but Bigod had to surrender in the face of a royal counter-attack. Alnodus the royal engineer and his carpenters and masons were paid to demolish Framlingham castle. The castle then probably consisted of what is now the Lower Court with a motte (mound for a look-out tower) on the site later occupied by the poorhouse, since excavations there have shown that it is built on very disturbed ground.

Eventually Hugh Bigod's son recovered his father's estate in the 1180s. Roger Bigod II rebuilt the castle in stone around the remains of his father's hall and chapel, adding towers and another hall. He remained loyal to king Richard I but not to John. Beseiged by John's foreign troops in 1216, the castle was surrendered after two days, the defeated garrison consisting of 26 knights, 20 sergeants (men-at-arms), 7 crossbowmen, a chaplain and three others. This averages out at four defenders for a tower and length of curtain wall together. Framlingham castle was once again restored to the Bigods. The last Bigod refused to go to Gascony to fight in 1297 while the king went to Flanders, maintaining he had no obligation unless the king was there in person. 'By God, sir Earl' said king Edward I, 'you shall go or hang'. 'By God, O King' said Roger Bigod IV, 'I will neither go nor hang'. And he didn't, but his title and estates went to the king on his death in 1307.

ENGLISH HERITAGE

What was a castle for?

The idea of the castle – a fortified residence for a relatively small number of people, which might also function as an administrative centre – was primarily a Norman innovation in England. Defence is as old as the hills, but people in the Saxon, Roman and earlier periods usually combined together to erect communal defences against their enemies. On the other hand, the castle was a symbol of lordship, of feudal domination, a consolidation of power holdings. Where the owner of a castle – king, baron or great magnate – had several far-flung estates, the castle was usually left in charge of a constable, resident with a small garrison (a watchman, porter and a few men-at-arms). When the owner arrived, the full accommodation would be opened up, but many of the entourage would have to live in tents or find rooms outside the castle in the nearest town or village.

The first castles built by the Normans were made of earth and timber, quickly put up using local materials and labour. The earth dug from the ditches would be piled up on the inner side and faced and topped with timber palisading. Stone walls took far more time and organization to put up than earthworks. Frequently the style of earthwork thrown up was a motte and bailey. The motte was a high mound supporting and protecting a watchtower, with a bailey enclosure attached to one side and containing the other buildings, the hall, kitchen, barracks, stables, storehouses and workshops.

The Mowbrays

Framlingham was administered through relatives of the king for most of the next century, until Thomas Mowbray was made duke of Norfolk by king Richard II in 1397. Mowbray was given Framlingham and other estates, but he died in exile and his son was executed for rebellion against king Henry V. His brother John was recognised as duke of Norfolk in 1425 and often lived at Framlingham castle as did his son and grandson in succession. Ann Mowbray was engaged to Richard, duke of York, one of the princes who mysteriously disappeared in the Tower of London, and through her the estate passed to the Howard family.

Coat of arms of the Howard family c1525, sculptured over the entrance to Framlingham Castle.
The 'quarterings' of the heraldic shield are illustrated below

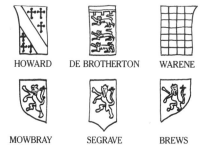

| HOWARD | DE BROTHERTON | WARENE |
| MOWBRAY | SEGRAVE | BREWS |

The Howards

John Howard repaired the royal castle before his death, when leading the royal army at the battle of Bosworth in 1485. His son was captured in the battle but restored to favour and made duke of Norfolk after successfully leading the new king's army in the battle of Flodden. Thomas Howard served his country by both land and sea. The Howard family monuments were in

ABOVE *Portrait of Thomas Howard, Duke of Norfolk, of about 1539*

Thetford priory, just over the Norfolk border. As part of the dissolution of the monasteries, Thetford priory was abandoned in 1540 and Thomas Howard rebuilt Framlingham church to house the tombs and monuments of his family. Unfortunately he crossed king Henry VIII. His son was executed, and he himself was only saved from the scaffold by the sudden death of Henry VIII on 23 January 1547, the night before his execution.

Queen Mary

In 1553, Framlingham castle was given by king Edward VI to his sister Mary. Here she waited that summer, while the succession to the crown hung in the balance. Her flag flew over the gateway and thousands of her supporters camped around Framlingham castle. The earl of Arundel arrived to tell Mary she was queen, and soon afterward the duke of Norfolk was freed from the Tower of London. In the time of Queen Elizabeth Framlingham castle was used as a prison for recusant priests (i.e. those defying the new Church of England) before being returned to the Howards in 1613. But the glory of Framlingham was over: the Howards preferred their new house at Kenninghall in Norfolk and the castle was leased out and finally sold to Sir Robert Hitcham in 1635.

RIGHT *Portrait of Queen Mary Tudor, dated 1544*

NATIONAL PORTRAIT GALLERY

19

PEMBROKE COLLEGE, UNIVERSITY OF CAMBRIDGE

ABOVE *Engraved portrait of Sir Robert Hitcham who died in 1636*

BELOW *Hitcham's Almshouses, Framlingham, as they are today*

ENGLISH HERITAGE

ABOVE *Framlingham Castle when it was first taken into state guardianship – from an old postcard*

Later History

Sir Robert Hitcham was a prominent lawyer in royal service and also a member of Parliament. He died in 1636, leaving Framlingham castle to be demolished (except its stone walls). The materials were used for almshouses and a school for forty poor boys from the parishes of Framlingham, Debenham and Coggeshall (Essex). Not surprisingly the lawyer's will caused great problems and it was nearly thirty years before matters were sorted out. The almshouses were built in Framlingham, and are there today on the road between the College and the Castle. The castle, fortunately for us, was not pulled down and in 1664, when the brick workhouse was erected, John Kilborne agreed to provide wool for 300 poor people to spin provided he was given a residence and a small salary. Children formed most of the inmates in 1699, when they were to be 'clothed in blew with bonnetts as at Christ Church Hospital and to have Sir Robert Hitcham's arms upon their coats.' The master of the poorhouse was 'every

day to give leave to each child two hours... to read, write or cast accomts as the School master think fittest.'

Some of the surviving stone buildings in the castle were used by the workhouse until they were pulled down in 1688. A sketch of them, with the brick house alongside, survives in the papers of Pembroke College, Cambridge. Later the children were apprenticed out and only adult paupers were housed in the castle. The present poorhouse was built in 1729 and became redundant in 1839 when a new workhouse was built at Wickham Market to serve the surrounding area, including Framlingham. The great hall was leased out for parish meetings and later as assembly rooms for meetings and dances. Just before Pembroke College gave the castle into State care in 1913, it was being used as a courtroom, drill hall for the local volunteers and parish fire station.

BELOW *Seventeenth-century sketch of the workhouse, which was partly pulled down in 1688*

English Heritage welcomes you to Orford Castle

Orford castle lies in the west of the Village, on the far side of the central open space (Market Hill) from the parish church and about a kilometre north-west of Orford Quay. The outer walls of the castle have gone, but impressive banks and ditches remain. The central keep is almost perfect. It is nearly 30 metres high, with a wonderful view from the top. Its eighteen sides and three square turrets contain a labyrinth of passages and rooms, all built about 1165-67.

Contents

For Framlingham Castle, please turn to page 2

Tour of Orford Castle

ENGLISH HERITAGE

In front of Orford castle are two 6-pounder muzzle-loading cannon, dating from about 1800. They were designed as the 'chase' or forward guns of a frigate. They are mounted on their modern carriages, copied from a naval pattern used for shore garrisons. The cannon are said to have come from Sudbourne Hall near Orford. Perhaps they were sent ashore as part of the coastal defences against the threat of Napoleonic invasion. There are some remains of a 'Martello' tower of the same date, north of Orford.

It was partly the threat of a much earlier invasion in the twelfth century which caused king Henry II to have Orford castle built between 1165 and 1173, when he began to build a new town here and improve the port by draining the marshes. Orford already had a market, but a new church was begun at the same time as the castle.

From the car park the shape of the **keep** or donjon (great Tower) can be seen. The three projecting square turrets have only narrow slit-windows to light their interiors but in the four panels of wall between each pair of turrets there are two pairs of windows, one above the other, which light the central halls within. The shapes and sizes of the various walls were carefully

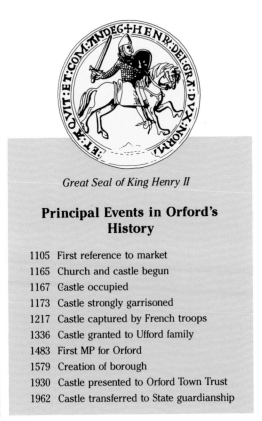

Great Seal of King Henry II

Principal Events in Orford's History

1105	First reference to market
1165	Church and castle begun
1167	Castle occupied
1173	Castle strongly garrisoned
1217	Castle captured by French troops
1336	Castle granted to Ufford family
1483	First MP for Orford
1579	Creation of borough
1930	Castle presented to Orford Town Trust
1962	Castle transferred to State guardianship

calculated to create harmony. Follow the path across the castle ditch and round to the right you reach the entrance, built to half the height of the rest in the corner between two turrets.

Three different kinds of stone were used to build the castle. Most of the walls are made of roughly-cut blocks of local clayey limestone (septaria) which erodes badly. For finer work a sandy oolite was brought from Northampton-shire by river and sea, and for the finest work of all, mainly on the inside of the keep, a fine cream-coloured limestone was brought from Caen in Normandy. Henry II was duke of Normandy as well as king of England.

Entrance

The steps up to the door are not very old, but they follow the line of the original ones. The rectangular doorcase too is fairly modern, but the low triangular arch above, its stones joggled together like those in the entrance to Framlingham castle (page 13) is Norman. The group of holes in the turret high above your head (see photograph on right) are the flues from the kitchen fireplaces you will see inside.

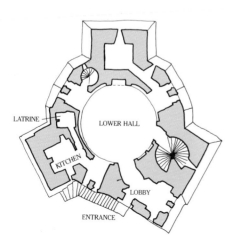

Inside the keep door is a triangular **lobby**, where the porter could question visitors and arrange or prevent their entry into the main part of the keep. Immediately below the lobby, and reached now by a steep staircase, is a cell fitted with a ventilation shaft and a latrine passage in the space under the entrance stairs. This could have been for the porter's use, tied as he was to a fixed point of duty, but equally it could be used as a prison. Medieval prisoners were only useful if they were kept alive, so basic sanitation would have been necessary, if only to prevent an epidemic from killing everyone living in the keep.

ABOVE *Looking up from below the entrance. The five small holes at the top left are smoke vents from the kitchen fireplaces*

LEFT *The entrance doorway has a triangular-headed arch like Framlingham (see page 13)*

24

The main **entrance** to the keep proper has round arches fanning out on to ornamental carved **capitals** (supporting stone blocks) on one side but not on the other, as the picture shows. There were inner doors which closed against the next two triangular-headed arches pictured here. These doors were bolted shut by great wooden bars which would be slid out of their long sockets in the sides of the arches across the opening into shallower sockets on the other side. As you can see, one bar slid one way, the other in the opposite direction. As the next photograph shows, people carved their names on Orford castle 300 years ago – but don't add yours!

Orford castle was designed as a fortified family home, which could if necessary accommodate a larger gathering. For example important visitors could be housed, a criminal or manorial court held, or a council of war. The 'family' might be royal – the king or his representative with a glittering entourage – or, more humbly, a salaried castellan with a minimal staff of a watchman, porter and a few men-at-arms.

The thick walls of the castle are riddled with rooms and passages. You should imagine them hung with cloths, plastered and painted, fitted with wooden doors and moveable furniture. Much of the time the hangings would be stored away and only parts of the castle inhabited. But clearly the castle was planned to provide comfortable living – at least by Norman standards!

Lower Hall

The circular room shown in the picture on the right has a stone bench all the way round except in front of the fireplace. A large number of people could sit or stand here, for a meeting or a meal. The **Hall** is well lit by daylight, in contrast to the small rooms elsewhere which we shall see. As the photograph on page 28 shows, the window recesses are slightly pointed at the top. The round 'Norman' style of arch was giving way to the pointed 'Gothic' shape just at this time when Orford castle was being built.

The **spiral stair** which links all the floors of the keep is on the right of the entrance. If you want to explore every passage as you go, the secret is to work your way round each hall clockwise, and then you won't miss anything.

Using this rule, you will find that the side passage opening off the window recess to the left of the entrance doorway leads you into a **kitchen**, with a shallow stone sink basin and two fireplaces. A further passage runs to a two-seat **latrine** (often called a garderobe, which really means a cupboard). As you can see, these

ABOVE *Triangular and round arches to the inner door. Note the ornamented capitals on which they rest*

LEFT *Graffiti on the side of the doorway*

LOWER LEFT *Window recess in lower hall, with stone bench. Note stairs leading up to wall-passage*

BELOW *Two-seat latrine. The wall separating the cubicles has been demolished, leaving a scar on the wall*

A reconstruction illustration of the keep as it might have appeared in the twelfth century

ENGLISH HERITAGE

latrines are ventilated and lit quite well by medieval standards. Originally they opened directly off the hall, and the passage may have been made to allow more privacy. From the next window recess a stair spirals up to a private room, past the triangular urinal drain shown in the picture on the far right.

Beyond the **fireplace**, which had to be large to heat a room this size, another side passage from the window leads straight into another private room below that just mentioned. The plaster above the windows here and elsewhere in the keep shows the marks of the wooden planks which were used to support the stone arches while the mortar was drying. Glass was rare in the Norman period, and the window openings would normally have been open in daylight, but closed by shutters against the weather. The fireplace (and another one in the hall above) indirectly kept these private rooms warm also.

The final opening, to the left of the entrance as you look back, leads to the wide spiral staircase, going both down to the basement and up to the upper hall and roof. Like most defensive staircases it rises clockwise. An attacker climbing such a stair could not wield a sword in his right hand properly. A defender standing above him would be at a distinct advantage.

out on its own. The well water would probably have been a bit salty, with the sea so near. Rainwater from the roof was stored in the keep, as we shall see. Such a large basement must have been used for storage, particularly of food. Any prisoners kept here would have interfered with access to the well, even if they didn't pollute it.

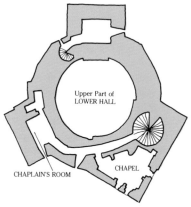

Chapel

If you go back up the spiral staircase, past the entrance to the lower hall, the next passage on the left leads off first into a triangular chapel above the entrance lobby. The drawing below shows its altar with a cupboard and sink (for the

ABOVE *Norman urinal in the wall of the passage*

ABOVE *The spiral staircase. Note the marks in the mortar overhead where wooden boards held the mortar until it dried*

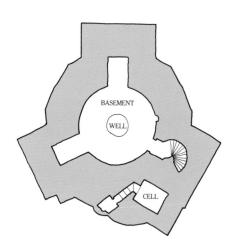

Basement

Go down the staircase first of all to the circular basement of the keep. The wall recesses form storage rooms in the base of the keep turrets, and between them are slits sloping up to let in daylight from high up in the walls. Castle basements are usually dark, without large openings in the walls through which attackers could force their way into the keep. The large **well** in the middle is about ten metres deep. Coupled with a food store, the keep could hold

ABOVE *A reconstruction illustration of the chapel as it may have appeared originally*

ABOVE *Drain from kitchen sink*

ABOVE *Upper Hall fireplace. Projecting stones supported the beams. See reconstruction illustration on opposite page*

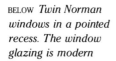

BELOW *Twin Norman windows in a pointed recess. The window glazing is modern*

celebration of Holy Communion) alongside. There are arches of brownish oolite and white Caen stone round the walls, with capitals carved with Norman patterns, but here and there they do not seem to match up. Was there some change of plan? As you leave the chapel, notice the narrow gap at the edge of the floor to the left of the door. This marks the slot in which the **portcullis** rose and fell, although it is blocked now by the modern doorcase below. A portcullis was an iron-bound grating which could be lowered (often behind an ordinary door, as here) to block an entrance completely. A door might be forced open, but a portcullis had to be levered upwards, or the masonry round its edges broken away, which was a far more difficult job. When not in use, the portcullis would have hung from its ropes and pulleys against the chapel wall.

If you continue along the passage you reach the **chaplain's room**, with his store-room and latrine beyond. All the castle drains are concentrated in this part of the walls, and we shall see how they were arranged outside.

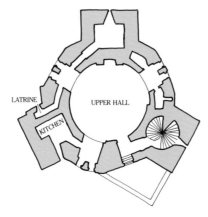

Upper Hall

Return along the passage and go up the spiral stair further. The next passage forked left to the roof of the chapel (not now accessible to visitors) and right into the upper hall. This is generally similar to the lower hall, except that there is no stone bench round the walls. The large stones projecting at intervals all the way round from the walls are corbels, which supported the bottom of the beams which formed the original conical roof, shown in the reconstruction illustrations on pages 26 and 29. The doorways which you can see high up in the walls lead to chambers in the turrets reached by a catwalk between and above the original conical roof and the castle walls. As the cross-section shows, this roof would have been hidden behind the parapets and turrets and so it would not have been exposed to missiles or

fire-arrows thrown by the besiegers. Like that in the hall below, the first recess to the left of the entrance from the stair leads into a kitchen with its own double fireplace and drain, as shown on far left. The next window recess is a variation on the one below, in that there is a latrine to the left and a private lodging to the right. Well-ventilated cupboards (true garderobes) open off each side of the third window. Displayed on the walls are copies of Tudor maps of Orford, with sketches of the castle keep and its surrounding walls and towers which have now vanished. John Norden's drawing of the castle in 1600, is reproduced on page 33.

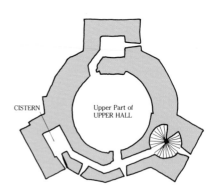

Still climbing upward, you reach another wall-passage which leads past a high doorway (one of those accessible from the former catwalk above the conical roof just described) to a lined **cistern**. This would have been filled with rainwater collected from the catwalk gutter, and would have been preferable to the brackish water from the well in the basement. Also, it is easier to carry a bucket downstairs than up. King Henry II's keep at Dover actually had a piped water supply fed by just such a cistern, some twenty years later.

Roof

The staircase ends at the modern flat roof, with three turrets rising higher, each with a stone rainwater spout venting inwards and so supplying the cistern. The tops of the turrets are not open to visitors (originally they must have been fighting and watch-platforms reached by ladders). The turret on the right contains an oven and baking-chamber, partly floored with glazed tiles. This was not for decoration but was a practical way of using floor-tile 'wasters'

RIGHT *A feast in the Upper Hall of Orford Castle, from the reconstruction illustration by Alan Sorrell*

ENGLISH HERITAGE

(which had been fired to a high temperature but had distorted in the process) here where uneven heating would occur in the baking process. In the same way, the oven roof contains many ordinary clay rooftiles. The patterns on the floor-tiles (perhaps the earliest visible in England today) are shown in the drawing on the right.

The other turret still has its original battlements, with plaster protecting some of the stonework against erosion in the salt air. As at Framlingham, the holes which can be seen in the sides of the **crenels** (gaps in the battlements) were for the iron pivots of horizontal shutters. These shutters protected the defenders who, if they wanted to see or shoot out, would push the

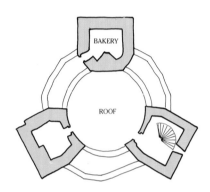

shutter upwards and outwards, letting it fall back when they had finished.

But the main reason for climbing to the top of the keep is for the magnificent view, particularly seawards over Orford Ness. In front is the river Alde, rising many miles behind you and flowing almost to the sea at Aldeburgh (on the coast to your left) and then for miles parallel to the sea before finally joining it (as the river Ore) to your right. The view, from left to right, shows:

☐ The mast broadcasting the BBC World Service
☐ The church tower, recently rebuilt. It acted as a sea-mark before the series of lighthouses on Orford Ness were built.
☐ The present red-and-white banded lighthouse is automatically operated, and can be seen for 25 kilometres out to sea in good weather.
☐ The hangar and 'pagodas' have had various military uses. In World War I the Ness was an airfield, in World War II it was used for ballistic experiments and later for the Cobra Mist radio research project.

OPPOSITE PAGE *Orford Castle from the air, with its earthwork defences in front of the keep, and the church and coast behind*

☐ Havergate Island, to the right, is a bird sanctuary famous for its avocets.

Turning round and looking inland, in the foreground you can see the banks and ditches which defended the castle to landward. Under the hawthorn bushes to the left are the foundations of part of the stone outer defences. Much of the forest here on the 'Sandlings' has a long history. Staverton Thicks, on the way to Woodbridge, contains stands of old coppiced oak trees. Timber, like anything which grows, can be cropped. Staverton was a deerpark in the Middle Ages. The monks of Butley Priory took the Queen of France here for a picnic in 1524. Today their successors, the Forestry Commission, provide picnic sites for their visitors too. Just before Woodbridge, to the left, is Sutton Hoo, the site of the great Saxon ship-burial whose treasures can be seen in the British Museum (and copies in the Ipswich Museum if you don't want to go that far).

If you turn right at the foot of the steps on leaving the keep, the group of shoots from the latrines can be seen pictured below, with the kitchen drain spouts directly above which would have served to flush them. This is typical of the detailed design of this remarkable keep, which packs comfort and privacy around sizeable halls, all within protective defences. An octagonal keep also built for king Henry II at Chilham in Kent has been modernised inside and now forms a luxury home.

ABOVE RIGHT *Patterns in the floor-tiles incorporated into the baking-chamber*

ABOVE LEFT *Baking-chamber (on right) and firehole (left) in the north turret*

LEFT *Latrine outfalls at the foot of the castle wall*

Town

From the castle a very pleasant walk can be had by way of the wide market-place surrounded by old houses of various styles, to the parish church, with its original Norman chancel now in ruins, which was begun at the same time as the castle. Turn right, and walk downhill to Orford Quay. Orford was both a market town and a port in the twelfth century, but ships found it more and more difficult to sail up the river because of silting, and Orford declined until the seventeenth century when the fishing industry prospered. The Tudor maps in the keep show fixed boats in the river which were used for fishing.

Orford is on the estuary of the river Alde which rises near Framlingham and flows to Aldeburgh, where it is deflected by a long shingle spit which is growing by about 15 metres a year and extends now 10 kilometres beyond Orford. Before the lighthouse was built on Orford Ness, ships used the church tower and the castle as sea-marks for navigation. Norden's drawing opposite shows the beacon light on the castle. This could be used either for navigation or for warning of invasion.

The area is well-known to naturalists for its wildfowl, wading birds and flowers: yellow horned poppies, purple flowering sea pea, sea kale, sea lavender and sea purslane are all growing here. Inland, red deer and red squirrels inhabit the forests.

BELOW *Orford Castle, town and the Alde estuary, from the estate plan by John Norden, dated 1602. Note the fisherman's huts on the shingle (bottom right) and small boats permanently moored*

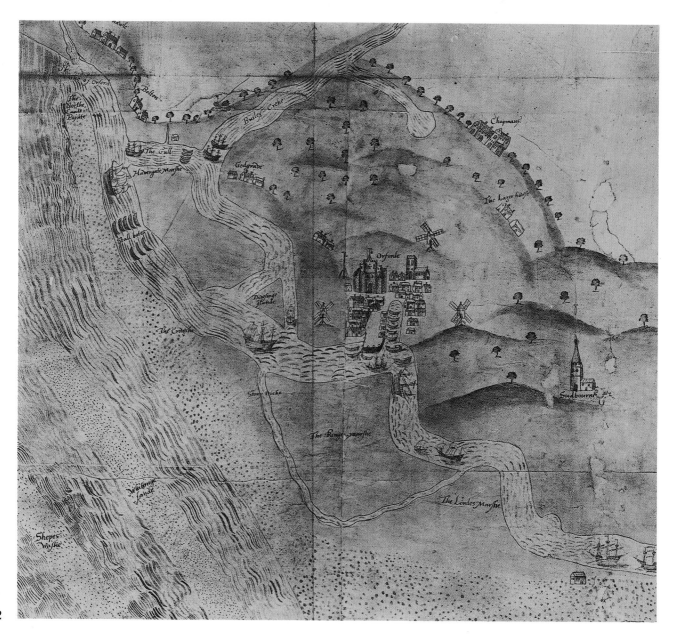

CASTRI ORFORDENSIS IN ORIENTEM PROSPECTVS.

ABOVE *Orford Castle in 1600, showing the outer walls (now destroyed) and the old church tower (on right)*

History of Orford Castle

Orford castle is remarkable, not only because of its unique shape and planning, but also because it is the earliest castle whose entire building accounts survive (in the Public Record Office in London). Over the period from 1165 to 1173 a total of £1413 was spent on the castle, most of it in the first two years. This sounds ridiculously cheap today, but don't forget that inflation has always been with us. In the twelfth century a watchman received an (old) penny a day for wages, the king's constable perhaps £20 a year and the whole royal revenues were less than £10,000 a year. Also there is evidence that some costs were set off against local debts and taxes in cash and kind without going through the central accounting system. Local men certified the expenditure, including the chaplain of the new church then being a-building and Bartholomew de Glanville. He was to be the first constable of Orford from 1167, by which time supplies were being ordered, so the castle must have been habitable. It seems that the keep was built first, followed by the curtain walls and towers and finally the ditches and palisading. Bartholomew was in charge when a merman was caught off the coast (see page 35).

As well as building the castle, king Henry II was improving the port by draining the marshes and building the church. Why all this interest? The answer lies at Framlingham, some way inland from Orford. Henry II was concerned to reduce the power of his barons, particularly their holdings of castles. In East Anglia the main threat was Hugh Bigod, earl of Norfolk (which meant Suffolk too at that time) who held the castles of Bungay, Framlingham, Thetford and Walton, and claimed the royal castle of Norwich as well. The only royal castles between Colchester and Norwich were small inland ones at Eye and Haughley. In 1157, Hugh Bigod was required to surrender all his castles to king

The builder of Orford and his wife

King Henry II

When king Henry I died in 1135, there followed nearly 20 years of civil war between Stephen and Maltilda, who were the grandchildren of William the Conqueror. Eventually Stephen agreed to Maltilda's son, Henry of Anjou, becoming heir to the throne. He was crowned Henry II.

King Henry II ruled an empire stretching from Scotland to southern France and he brought Ireland under the English crown. He was an able administrator and man of action, but was worn down by the rebellions of his children who were supported by the king of France.

The first rebellion, shortly after Henry's fatal quarrel with his archbishop Thomas Becket, had led to the capture of the king of Scotland and of an invasion of Flemings led by the earl of Leicester. Landing at Walton, the Flemings were ambushed near Bury St Edmunds by local and royal forces. A second landing, intended to link up with Hugh Bigod, was not followed up.

Queen Eleanor

Eleanor was the heiress to the duchy of Aquitaine in south-western France, who married Louis VII, king of France (that is, the region around Paris) in 1137. The marriage produced daughters only and the couple divorced in 1151. Eleanor rapidly married Henry of Anjou; soon to be king of England and already duke of Normandy.

She bore Henry four sons, but by 1170 they were separated, she living in her duchy in the south, the patroness of knights and troubadours, of tournaments and chivalry. When she actively supported her sons' revolt against their father Henry II, the king placed her under 'open arrest' for 15 years until his death. For the remaining 15 years of her life, she played a dominant role in the reigns of her sons Richard I and John.

ABOVE *The drawings are from the effigies of Henry II and Eleanor in Fontevrault Abbey (near Saumur in the Loire Valley) where both are buried*

BELOW *Henry II with Thomas Becket, from a thirteenth-century manuscript*

BRITISH LIBRARY

CASTLE MUSEUM, NORWICH

Orford Castle and village in 1856, as painted by Henry Bright

Henry II. Henry clearly intended that his new castle at Orford should control the coast. He may have begun it even before 1165 (when he started repaying the expenditure upon it) since in that year he returned Bungay and Framlingham to Bigod in exchange for a large fine. Henry however kept Walton castle (on the coast near Felixstowe) until Orford was complete and then demolished it.

The Orford Merman

The story, as told by Ralph of Coggeshall, writing about 1207 but referring to a time about forty years earlier, reads as follows:

'Men fishing in the sea caught in their nets a wild man. He was naked and was like a man in all his members, covered with hair and with a long shaggy beard. He eagerly ate whatever was brought to him but if it was raw he pressed it between his hands until all the juice was expelled. He would not talk, even when tortured and hung up by his feet. Brought into church, he showed no signs of reverence or belief. He sought his bed at sunset and always remained there until sunrise.

He was allowed to go into the sea, strongly guarded with three lines of nets, but he dived under the nets and came up again and again. Eventually he came back of his own free will. But later on he escaped and was never seen again.'

But Orford alone could not defend the whole coast. When Henry II's eldest son rebelled against his father, he was abetted by Bigod and by Flemish mercenaries who were landed near Orford. But the rebellion collapsed and Framlingham castle was demolished. (For its rebuilding and the later history of the Bigods, see page 17). Orford had been heavily reinforced with men (to judge from their wage bill) and supplies. Bacon, cheese and salt were brought in together with coal, iron, tallow, ropes and handmills. Houses from the town were dismantled and brought in to provide more accommodation.

In 1217 Orford castle was captured by Louis, the French leader during the fighting after the death of king John. Thereafter the castle was repaired from time to time but from 1280 onwards it was granted out and eventually sold. Until then it had performed the function of a centre of local government and the symbol of royal authority at an important, if declining, port. The estuary silted up and trade declined. Orford was a borough from 1579 to 1886 and was represented in Parliament at least from 1483 to 1832. An earldom of Orford existed for a time: the most famous earl was Sir Robert Walpole, prime minister for 21 years. In 1930 the remains of the castle were presented to the Orford Town Trust by Sir Arthur Churchman, and in 1962 it passed into State guardianship

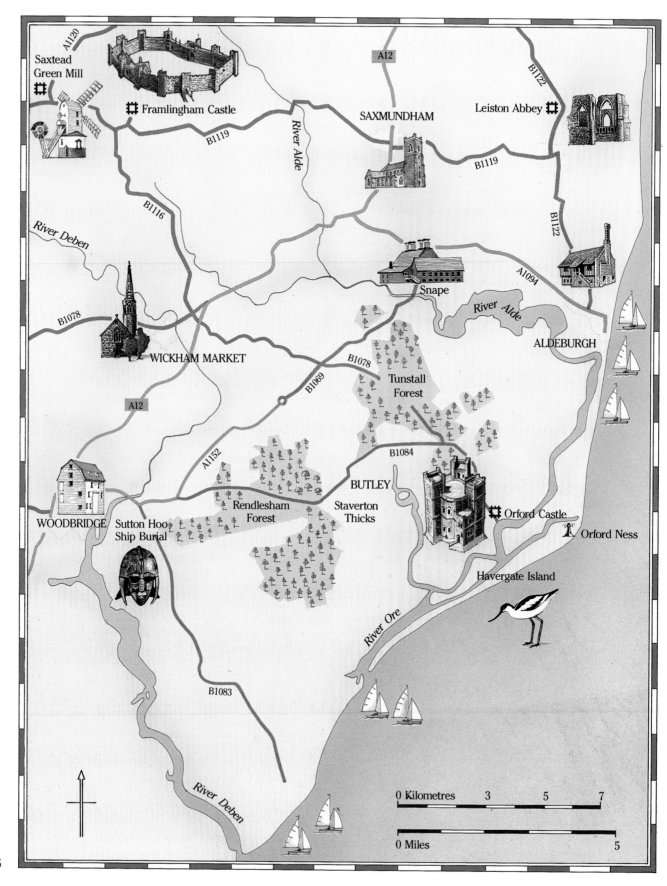

Saxtead
Green Mill

A1120

Framlingham Castle

A12

B1122

Leiston Abbey

SAXMUNDHAM

B1119

River Alde

B1119

B1116

River Deben

B1122

B1078

A1094

Snape

River Alde

WICKHAM MARKET

ALDEBURGH

B1078

B1069

Tunstall
Forest

A12

A1152

B1084

BUTLEY

Rendlesham
Forest

Staverton
Thicks

Orford Castle

WOODBRIDGE

Sutton Hoo
Ship Burial

Orford Ness

Havergate Island

River Ore

B1083

River Deben

| 0 Kilometres | 3 | 5 | 7 |

| 0 Miles | | | 5 |